Community Organising

The **UK** *Context*

Paul Henderson, Harry Salmon

GN00802135

COMMUNITY DEVELOPMENT FOUNDATION
• PUBLICATIONS •

**CHURCHES COMMUNITY
WORK ALLIANCE**

First published in Great Britain in 1995 by
Community Development Foundation
60 Highbury Grove
London N5 2AG
in association with
Churches Community Work Alliance
The Co-ordinating Secretary
36 Sandygate
Wath-upon-Dearne
Rotherham S63 7LW

Cover design by Edward Bear Associates, Amsterdam
Typeset by Stanford Desktop Publishing Services, Milton Keynes
Printed in Great Britain by Crowes of Norwich

British Library Cataloguing-in-Publication Data
A record of this publication is available from the British Library.

ISBN 0 902406 96 5

Contents

Community Development Foundation

The Community Development Foundation (CDF) was set up in 1968 to pioneer new forms of community development.

CDF strengthens communities by ensuring the effective participation of people in determining the conditions which affect their lives. It does this through:

* providing support for community initiatives
* promoting best practice
* informing policy-makers at local and national level.

As a leading authority on community development in the UK and Europe, CDF is a non-departmental public body and is supported by the Voluntary Services Unit of the Home Office. It receives substantial backing from local and central government, trusts and business.

CDF promotes community development through:

* local action projects
* conferences and seminars
* consultancies and training programmes
* research and evaluation services
* parliamentary and public policy analysis
* information services
* *CDF News*, a quarterly newsletter
* publications.

Chairman: Alan Haselhurst, MP
Chief Executive: Alison West

Community Development Foundation
60 Highbury Grove
London N5 2AG
Tel: 0171 226 5375
Fax: 0171 704 0313
Registered Charity Number 306130

Churches Community Work Alliance

Established in 1990, the Alliance is a partnership of churches, large childcare voluntary agencies and networks of church-related community work practitioners in England, Ireland, Scotland and Wales. Its objectives are to:

- support and encourage individual and collective vocations and initiatives for community work in the life and mission of the Churches
- contribute theological insights relevant to the Churhes' mission and involvement in community work of all kinds and their response to social and economic change
- foster and develop good community work practice
- provide guidance for community work projects.

Churches Community Work Alliance
Revd Brian Ruddock
Co-ordinating Secretary
CCWA
36 Sandygate
Wath-upon-Dearne
Rotherham S63 7LW
Tel and Fax: 01709 87 3254

Preface

Our purpose in writing this booklet is to place Community Organising – experiences of the movement in America and its development in Britain – within the context of community development in the UK. We do not intend to provide a full critique of the subject – its pros and its cons – or to explore its theological implications. Our interest is in communicating its history and main elements to those people who work in the community but who have had little or no contact with Community Organising. At the same time we seek to explore questions which are raised by the introduction of the concept to the UK.

Our impression is that there is interest among community workers in engaging in a debate on Community Organising in the UK. How does it relate to 'home-grown' practice models? Does it provide a basis for challenging the political ideology which, at any one time, is dominant? These kinds of questions are being asked, and our hope is that this booklet will help to clarify differences – of context and practice – between the USA and UK, to promote a constructive debate and lead to the sharing of experience between all those involved in work at the grassroots.

Our approach has been to reflect upon Community Organising at one step removed from its activities. The sources of our material are secondary – publications and unpublished papers – and we have made use of these alongside our own and others' experiences and understanding of community development. As a result, our focus is upon raising questions as opposed to putting forward conclusions based on empirical investigation. Our hope is that this kind of contribution will be the precursor to a greater interchange of experiences and ideas between those involved in Community Organising, and community workers and local people who form part of the 'tradition' of community development and community action in the UK.

Since Community Organising became established in the UK in the late 1980s, there has been a reluctance on the part of key participants to enter into discussion with those who might have reservations about certain of its aspects. There has been an understandable emphasis upon concentrating on working with those who accept the principles of Community Organising and who are prepared to work for their implementation. However, while the movement's commitment to 'action' rather than 'talk' is commendable, it can also alienate some who share the same sense of outrage at the injustices in our society and who are seeking ways to empower the powerless.

Our intention has been to present a balanced appraisal of Community Organising, but the expression of this intention was not sufficient to persuade key actors in the early stages of developing Community Organising to have any conversation with us about this publication. We still hope to have produced a fair assessment, but are more than ready to listen to and learn from readers' comments.

We are grateful to the Joseph Rowntree Charitable Trust for supporting the publication of this booklet and to the following individuals for reading and advising us on early drafts: Richard Farnell, Rob Furbey, Richard Hallett, Stevie Krayer, Geoff Marsh, Stephen Pittam, David Thomas and Alison West.

The booklet is published jointly by the Community Development Foundation and the Churches Community Work Alliance. Responsibility for its content, however, is ours alone.

Paul Henderson
Harry Salmon

Abbreviations

ACORN	Association of Community Organisations for Reform Now
AMA	Association of Metropolitan Authorities
BCC	British Council of Churches
COGB	Communities Organised for Greater Bristol
COF	Citizen Organising Foundation
CUF	Church Urban Fund
IAF	Industrial Areas Foundation
IJR	Institute of Juvenile Research
Mgr	Monsignor
MBO	Merseyside Broad-Based Organising
RC	Roman Catholic
UK	United Kingdom
UPA	Urban Priority Area
USA	United States of America

The authors have used the term Community Organising throughout, even though some individuals and agencies use the term Broad-Based Organising.

1   Church and Community

During the last 25 years or so the churches have become increasingly involved in community work. This started in a modest way at the end of the 1960s with the setting up of projects in inner-city areas. The process gained momentum in the 1970s and 1980s. Church-based community workers, for example, were supported by the then British Council of Churches Community Work Unit, the Gulbenkian Foundation funded a number of church community work projects, and Social Responsibility Officers pioneered significant developments. However, it was as a result of the recommendations of the Archbishop of Canterbury's Commission (1985) in *Faith in the City*, and the consequent setting up by the Church of England of the Church Urban Fund (CUF), that expansion took place. The existence of the CUF enabled community work projects to be established in Urban Priority Areas during the latter half of the 1980s. Other denominations – notably the United Reformed Church – were also seeing community work as a legitimate way of establishing contact with people living in areas of urban deprivation.

However, since the mid-1980s a new element has been introduced into the involvement of the churches in communities. A number of church leaders and people concerned with church-related community work began to visit the USA to familiarise themselves with the principles and practice of Community Organising. This is a way of working with people dating back to the late 1930s when Saul Alinsky organised residents of a predominantly Irish white Chicago neighbourhood. He went on in 1940 to set up the Industrial Areas Foundation (IAF), and it is this body which continues to promote Community Organising. The IAF, along with other advocates of Community Organising, has acted as host to many visitors from the UK, and some of them have come back committed to seeing Community Organising adopted in their country.

Why should there be this interest in Community Organising? What has given rise to this enthusiasm for a method of working which was first developed on the other side of the Atlantic more than 50 years ago?

Undoubtedly, concern over the growing powerlessness of ordinary people, anger because of the growth of inequalities in society, combined with frustration induced by the ineffectiveness of traditional community work responses, have prompted an urgent search for ways in which citizens can begin to fight back. For many years now, the most oppressed sections of society have had little faith in the ballot box as a way of achieving change. We are now beginning to see this scepticism becoming more general. There is also mounting cynicism about the never-ending succession of special programmes which are paraded by governments as being responses to the ills of society.

In the late 1960s there was a growing belief that change could be achieved by ordinary people. The US Civil Rights Movement and the 1968 uprisings seemed to show that 'power to the people' could be more than a slogan. During the early 1970s there was a rapid expansion in the UK of various forms of community work, and community action began to be seen as a way in which poor and deprived people could begin to gain some control over their own situations. The hopes of the 1960s were never fulfilled. Community workers began to modify their expectations of what they could achieve, and at the same time the political climate in which change had to be achieved became colder.

In 1985, the Archbishop of Canterbury's Commission on Urban Priority Areas published its report showing how government policies had widened the gulf between expanding bands of the very rich and the very poor, between the residents of 'comfortable Britain' and those who lived in inner-city areas and rundown estates. The report prompted a stream of criticisms from government ministers and, on the other hand, stirred many churches into establishing community work projects in disadvantaged areas. Prior to the report, the childcare voluntary organisations – Save the Children, NCH – Action for Children, Barnardo's and The Children's Society – had begun to devote more of their resources to setting up community-based projects.

And yet little changed. Community work remained peripheral to dealing with the inequalities documented in *Faith in the City*. Poor people continued to be powerless and, if anything, the gap between rich and poor continued to widen.

It was against this background that a number of concerned people – most of them with experience of community work in the UK – began to look to America for inspiration. James Pitt, a community worker, and Maurice Keane, a former Jesuit priest with experience of the inner city, had blazed a trail to the USA as early as 1981 at the invitation of Mgr Jack Egan, a Chicago priest and a long-standing friend of Saul Alinsky. Egan's response to the failure of community work to make any significant impact in Britain was to say 'you've never really tried it. Come to the USA and see how it is done.' Keane and Pitt accepted the invitation, and have provided us with a written account of their experience (Pitt and Keane, 1984).

Since then a succession of fieldworkers, charitable fund administrators and church leaders have been to the USA. They have visited projects, met with IAF officials and participated in their training programmes. Not all of them have been involved in building a movement in the UK, but many were impressed by what they saw, and some have been persuaded that Community Organising offers a way forward to achieve change by empowering the powerless.

Are they right? Does the concept offer a way forward? Or does it have a more modest contribution to make to our understanding of the principles and practice of working with communities?

Before we address these questions, we need to explore what Community Organising is. In order to do that, we have to go back to its founder, Saul Alinsky, and summarise the development of Community Organising in the USA.

2   'Produced in America'

As a nation, the UK imports too much. We have a similar tendency when it comes to trading in ideas across the Atlantic. Because Britons and Americans speak the same language, we imagine that approaches which appear to have worked 'over there' will also work 'over here'. In the early 1970s, the government-sponsored Community Development Projects borrowed freely from the American War on Poverty Programmes. During the same period, social work courses were eagerly importing the 'unitary approach' from American gurus. When it comes to urban regeneration, Glasgow looks to Baltimore, and local authorities searching for ways to revive their ailing urban economies have traded in the Boston market of ideas. The government has been attracted by America's 'minimal welfare' society, and has now begun to experiment with the privatisation of prisons.

British and American churches have long traded ideas and traditions. In the early 1960s, for example, Bruce Kenrick's account of the Protestant Churches initiative in East Harlem influenced developments in inner-city ministry in the UK (Kenrick, 1962).

The limitations of some of the market-led notions of regeneration have quickly been exposed, and other ideas have had a short shelf-life. But some ideas have taken root in the UK, and have been expressed in a form which has reflected their different social and cultural setting. Community Organising clearly bears the stamp 'produced in America', but does its development in that country afford any clues as to whether or not it will – to continue the 'root' metaphor – grow in our climate?

'Community organisation' was a dull piece of social work jargon until Saul Alinsky breathed life into it. Through his beliefs, thoughts and actions, he gave Community Organising an identity which it has retained, with only slight modifications, for more than 50 years.

Alinsky (1909–72) was born in a Jewish ghetto in Chicago to Orthodox Jewish parents. He graduated from the University of Chicago with an understanding of urban sociology, having shown through his fieldwork that he was a perceptive observer and that he had a remarkable capacity for establishing rapport with unlikely groups of people, including members of Chicago's notorious 'underworld'.

Back of the yards

On leaving university, Alinsky took a job as a sociologist in a prison, but he was too much of a rebel to survive for long as a worker in a penal institution. He had

4

worked under Clifford Shaw at the Institute of Juvenile Research (IJR) when he was a postgraduate student and in 1936 he resumed his association with Shaw. Now Shaw was setting up a project to demonstrate the links between delinquency and social conditions, and he was looking for a fieldworker to operate in a notorious district of Chicago known as Back of the Yards.

Back of the Yards was the location for slaughter houses, stockyards and the packing industry. The environment was foul, and the area was regarded as an industrial slum. Unemployment was running at almost 20 per cent, and there were high levels of delinquency. Half of the cosmopolitan population was Polish, and Catholic churches were strong. Irish people in the area were universally disliked because they were seen as occupying the positions of power. Alinsky was assigned to this district with the task of setting up a community committee, but his inclinations and early contacts were already beginning to move him in a different direction.

At the time when Alinsky started to work in Back of the Yards, a campaign to organise packing workers was in progress. The aim was to get employers to recognise the trade union. A national labour organisation had sent a group of professional organisers into Chicago, and Herb March, an inspirational member of the team, began to operate with the local Packinghouse Workers' Organising Committee. Alinsky was tremendously impressed by March and by the way that the task of organising the workers was tackled. He also noticed that at their meetings the activists did not restrict themselves to dealing with packing house issues but also raised questions relating to the community.

Herb March was one of Alinsky's first contacts, and an unsuccessful attempt to gun March down in December 1938 gave a new urgency to the formation of a neighbourhood committee. It also gave it a broader purpose and more political direction.

Alinsky had now become an organiser. In one of America's worst slums he was beginning to work out the principles on which Community Organising was to be based. Whereas Shaw had visualised a neighbourhood committee consisting of people serving as individuals, Alinsky created a committee composed of people who represented their constituencies (for example, churches and social groups). He searched out key people and, taking account of local tensions between different groups, carefully selected someone with a high level of acceptance to chair the first meeting of the neighbourhood council. For the next four months, Alinsky and Joe Meegan, the Chair of the council, spent their time preparing for their first public meeting.

The inaugural public meeting of the Back of the Yards Neighbourhood Council was held on a Friday night and was attended by 350 people representing 109 organisations. On the Sunday night there was to be a mass meeting of packing workers. Alinsky, who had already seen the tactical advantages of linking the establishment of a community organisation with the fight of the packing workers, had engineered a report in the local paper which linked the two things together. He was also instrumental in arranging for the popular auxiliary Roman Catholic Bishop of Chicago, Bernard Sheil, to address both gatherings.

The neighbourhood council gave its unanimous support to the packing workers in their campaign for trade union rights, and a delegation attended the mass meeting on the Sunday evening. Strike action was threatened, and the meat packaging companies gave in to the demands. *Time* magazine reported that the church, union and community had jointly achieved a victory. For the Back of the Yards Neighbourhood Council this was only the beginning.

Though this was Alinsky's first venture into Community Organising, it highlights a number of things which were to be the hallmarks of his approach throughout his life, many of which are still part of Community Organising as it is practised today.

As we have seen, his aim was to build a broadly based organisation made up of a wide range of groups from a defined geographical area. People did not serve as individuals, but as delegates from groups which had accepted a commitment to collective action. Back of the Yards also showed Alinsky's tactical skills. He was an opportunist. He saw that it was important for the new neighbourhood council to be associated with the packing workers' industrial dispute, not just because the issue appealed to his own sense of justice, but because he recognised that it was a focus for mass action. His skills were well demonstrated by his use of the press, by the way he got Bishop Sheil involved in both meetings and by ensuring that Joe Meegan became Chair of the neighbourhood council.

The churches and IAF

But one of the most significant features of this venture was its relationship with the churches. Much of the initial organising was done through the churches, and the support of key figures in the Roman Catholic Church was crucial. The link with the churches – and the RC Church in particular – was to remain a constant element in Alinsky's work, whereas his involvement with trade unions was to be transitory.

This relationship is all the more remarkable in that Alinsky was not a particularly religious person – he was not a practising Jew. He had a passionate commitment to oppressed people, but his own personal morality would have sometimes dismayed the devout. And yet he had the confidence, support and friendship of a number of prominent church leaders. Indeed, Bishop Shiel was to become one of the founder members of the IAF, and Alinsky's work was to be considerably helped by financial contributions from the RC Church. In his *Rules for Radicals* (1972), Alinsky referred to the Judaeo-Christian values which informed his own personal philosophy, and these values remain at the heart of IAF's work.

At the beginning of 1940, Saul Alinsky resigned from the IJR, and in September the IAF was established. Its board of trustees consisted of a small group of people committed to social reform, who believed that Alinsky could make a significant contribution to that process. Almost 60 years later the IAF is still in the business of Community Organising.

As requests came in – usually from groups of church leaders – for help in organising communities, Alinsky began to select and mould new organisers. The war and the tragic death of his first wife interrupted development of the work, but by the 1960s several neighbourhood organisations had been formed. However, the churches were not unanimous in their support for Alinsky and his methods.

At the end of the 1950s, while Alinsky was organising in another part of Chicago, Walter Kloetzli, a Lutheran pastor responsible for urban programmes, mounted an attack on him and his methods. He – like many other church leaders – found Alinsky's confrontational, mass action approach unacceptable. Protestants were often suspicious of the reasons for the deep involvement of Roman Catholics in Community Organising, and the movement became a divisive issue in many church forums. Sometimes ministers had to persuade reluctant congregations to give their support, and it was only the impact of the Civil Rights Movement which encouraged many black churches to become involved.

On the whole, it was the younger, more radical ministers of religion who saw in Alinsky's style of organising an opportunity for the churches to show their commitment to poor and oppressed people. As the spirit of ecumenism grew in the 1960s the involvement of the churches became more broadly based, but at higher administrative fund-dispensing levels it was the RC Church which continued to give the main support.

In spite of the conflicts generated within the churches about Community Organising, there is no doubt about the prominent contribution they made to the development of this method of intervention. It is the same today. In the mid-1970s the IAF reaffirmed its commitment to building organisations based upon local churches, and there are now something like a hundred such organisations. Ed Chambers, who was one of Alinsky's chosen organisers and who is the executive director of the IAF, says: 'We train people with the Bible, especially Moses and St Paul. They knew how to put an organisation together.' IAF's key asset is the high level of attendance at churches in the USA. It means that there is a constituency which can be accessed and mobilised relatively easily.

There has been a remarkable degree of continuity in the work of the IAF over the years. Its basic approach has remained largely the same, though since the 1970s there have been some changes of emphasis. More stress has been placed on ideology, values and political education, and an organisational network has been developed. The IAF has, however, held to its principles, and made no fundamental changes in its style of operating. Training continues to be based upon experience rather than upon textbooks, and the Foundation has refused any temptation to intellectualise its approach, though there is a greater willingness to engage in discussion with academics.

The IAF has shown that it is possible to create effective grassroots organisations in some of the most depressed urban areas, but whereas in the late 1930s Alinsky was on his own in pioneering this form of community action, since the early 1970s there has been a rapid growth in organisations seeking to empower ordinary people. They have drawn on a tradition of 'populism' in the USA, going back to the late nineteenth century when the Alliancemen formed the short-lived People's Party. The 'populists' advocated policies which stemmed from notions of mutuality, the common good and co-operation, and these values continue to survive in a society where there is also a strong attachment to a 'shoestring-to-riches' philosophy.

The result is that people in America are more inclined to become involved in locally based organisations than they are in the UK. Harry C. Boyte (1984) estimates that half of Americans devote an average of 17 hours a week to various forms of voluntary activity. In the UK, the periodic General Household Survey reveals that leisure time is increasingly non-communal As the conditions in which many Americans live have deteriorated, and people's faith in both the Republican and Democratic parties has declined, this willingness to become engaged in voluntary activity has found expression in a vast range of organisations concerned with giving ordinary people some influence over their local situations.

Other models

In assessing the appropriateness of the IAF model of Community Organising for the UK, it is important to take account of this cultural factor, and also to consider the possibility that there are other grassroots initiatives in the USA from which we can learn.

Delgado (1994) claims that there are now some 6,000 community organisations operating in the USA. Given the attention paid to the work of the IAF in the UK, we could be excused for imagining that this is the dominant North American approach to Community Organising. However, this is not the case. In a helpful analysis, Delgado identifies three different models of this form of community work in the USA. These are:

- the direct membership model
- the coalition model, and
- the institutionally-based model.

Though some organisations borrow from more than one model, there are others which clearly represent each different approach. The IAF is a prime example of the institutionally based approach, in that its community organisations are based mainly on church congregations.

If we are looking to North America for insights into effective Community Organising, then it is important to examine the different approaches which are being used. Below we describe two examples of this method of intervention, illustrating the direct membership model and the coalition model.

The Association of Community Organisations for Reform Now (ACORN) was founded in Little Rock, Arkansas, in 1970 to fight for the interests of 'low- and moderate-income' citizens. It was the first body to create a direct membership model capable of being adopted in a variety of situations, and it now has organisations made up of people on low incomes in 27 cities.

ACORN began as a project of the National Welfare Rights Organisation, but soon started to take up other issues which affected the least affluent sections of the population. It has always shown a readiness to adapt and change. In the early 1980s it was tackling the issue of homelessness in 15 cities by organising squats in empty properties. It also campaigned around issues such as bank lending policies and federal loan underwriting for people on low incomes.

Though it borrowed from Alinsky-style Community Organising, ACORN has always differed from it in a number of respects. We have already noted that its membership consists of individuals, not of institutional groups. From the beginning – unlike the IAF – it has been prepared to become involved in the political process, either by running candidates or supporting party candidates committed to representing the interests of low-income groups, and by dealing with agents of the civic authorities. Wade Rathke, one of ACORN's original organisers, is quoted as saying, 'Victories are won on the streets, but they are ratified at the polls.'

Whereas IAF operates in geographical areas to which it has been invited by a sponsoring group of church leaders, ACORN's constituency consists of 'low- and moderate-income' families. This means that it is less bound by physical boundaries, and has appreciated from the beginning the importance of initiating campaigns which cross city and state boundaries. It is more deserving of the description 'broad-based' Community Organising than the IAF's protégé in the UK, in that it does not subscribe to a restrictive Judaeo-Christian value base and it widens its membership through intensive door-knocking campaigns.

According to some commentators, Community Organising in the USA since the late 1970s has been tending to drift away from poor communities into organising more stable working- and middle-class communities. A similar trend can be discerned in this country. In America the exceptions to this are the new breed of independent organisations based on the identity of race, the National People's Action Network, and ACORN.

Over the years, ACORN has had its own internal tensions and policy disagreements, but these have arisen partly because it has been more flexible in its approach than the IAF. This has also been reflected in its attitude towards funding. Though it emphasises the importance of independent funding based upon individual membership dues, it is prepared to accept government grants for specific pieces of work. In the summer of 1993, ACORN used federal funding to finance a project in New York, in which young people from the homes of adult members informed residents of the dangers of lead paint and helped them to set up a committee to force city agencies to take action.

Citizen Action is a different kind of body from ACORN, though it has sometimes taken up similar issues. It is also committed to the wellbeing of people on low and moderate incomes. Though it is primarily based upon a coalition building model, some of the organisations associated with Citizen Action started as direct membership groups.

It began in 1970, and its first group was formed around the issue of pollution. Much of its work now consists of creating coalitions mainly based on senior citizen organisations, churches and trade unions. The focus of the coalitions will often be a combination of broad-based issues and support for progressive electoral candidates. Citizen Action has been particularly successful in linking issues affecting those on low and moderate incomes to electoral politics. In 1985 the radical Democrat, Tom Harkin, believed that the Iowa Citizen Action Network had played a crucial part in his election as a senator for that state.

According to Delgado, the training arm of Citizen Action has given considerable support to a number of women's projects. Generally the larger Community Organisations have neglected work with groups based on gender, race or sexual orientation.

Citizen Action obtains much of its financial support by soliciting donor contributions, holding house meetings and running money-raising events. However, the group, in common with other consultancy organisations, is finding funding an increasing problem.

This introduction to ACORN and Citizen Action serves to illustrate the different models of Community Organising. They underline the fact that there is a variety of approaches to the task of empowering people, and that if we are to learn from experience in the USA, then we might be wise not to limit our learning to any particular model.

3 The UK Picture

In this section we explore the development of Community Organising in the UK. We begin by asking why a number of experienced community workers and others became interested in the idea, and then explore the nature of the links that have been forged between the USA and UK.

Why the interest?
Curiosity
One explanation for the interest in Community Organising is that British community workers have received a flow of articles and booklets on the subject over the last 15 years. They have had their curiosity aroused, not least because of the movement's association with Alinsky who, on UK community work training courses, has often been put across as the hero of radical community action.

James Pitt and Maurice Keane published the report of their visit to the USA in 1984 – *Community Organising? You've Never Really Tried It!* In 1986 Alan Twelvetrees's article, 'Lessons from America – Alinsky's Legacy', appeared in the magazine *Community Care*, and in 1988 the *Christian Action Journal* devoted an entire issue to Community Organising, edited by Neil Jameson of the Citizen Organising Foundation (COF).

During the same period the Newcastle-based Research and Training Initiative organised two seminars on Community Organising. The tutors included Gary Delgado of ACORN, author of *Organising the Movement: The Roots and Growth of ACORN* (1986).

In 1990 Joe Hasler, writing in the British Council of Churches' *Issues in Church-Related Community Work*, raised some fundamental questions about Community Organising, and in 1991 Merseyside Churches' Urban Institute published *Broad Based Organising on Merseyside*, a wide-ranging report of a working party set up by Merseyside church leaders.

More recently there have been two substantive reports. Christian Action published *Community Organising: A Practical and Theological Appraisal* by Jay MacLeod (1993). And researchers from Coventry University, Sheffield Hallam University and the University of Sheffield produced an evaluation of Community Organising for the Church Urban Fund (Farnell et al., 1994).

These have been the most visible publications available in the UK. There have also been shorter articles and correspondence and many informal discussions

11

among community workers at regional and national conferences. As a result, information about Community Organising has flowed outside networks of church-related community work to lay organisations. Yet it has been a partial flow of information, enough to whet the appetite but thin on substance and with little analysis of how the initiative relates to community development. Consequently many people still have questions: what is Community Organising really about? Are there evaluative studies of its effectiveness in the USA? Are its values, methods and tactics compatible with those of community development? The interest is there because practitioners are in the position of looking over the shoulder of Community Organising. They want to know more.

Church community work

The political impact of *Faith in the City* (Archbishop of Canterbury's Commision, 1985) is widely acknowledged. Within the Church of England, implementation of the report's recommendation for a Church Urban Fund enabled a large number of community work projects to be initiated. A new energy was apparent. At one point the Church of England was said to employ the largest number of community workers in the country. As indicated earlier, other denominations showed a determination to respond to the high levels of poverty and unemployment in Britain's inner cities and peripheral estates by supporting community projects.

In many such projects, however, there was a lack of clarity as to the principles which should inform their work. *Faith in the City* had launched a commitment but had not come forward with a methodology:

> 'It said such a church should be local, open to the community, participative in style and ecumenical but it did not say how such a church could be created, what skills and knowledge it would require and how lay men and women could acquire them' (Austin, 1989, p. 68).

The emergence of Community Organising in the UK context held the promise of a model which could be adapted by church and community workers. The fact that the UK end of Community Organising seemed to have the active interest and support of a number of church leaders – as well as grants, in England, from the CUF – could provide significant recognition of the new approach. There was, therefore, an attentive audience waiting to learn from those people with knowledge and experience of the approach and based in projects where the approach could be tried. Perhaps the fact that church community projects and the development of Community Organising coincided helped create the climate of interest in the latter.

Despair

The appearance of Community Organising in the UK came at a time when community development was having to cope with the ideology and policies of the

Thatcher government. For most community workers this was a bewildering, exhausting and depressing experience.

There have been two dominant themes in British society with which community development has had to contend. One has been increased centralisation of policymaking and resource allocation. The effect of this has been to set boundaries to the meaning of democracy and the constituent elements of citizenship. The other theme has been the impact throughout society of the enterprise culture. The effect of this on community development has been to align it more closely with economic development, regeneration and enterprise at the expense of its links with social welfare and education.

In addition to the various government initiatives having an over-riding interest in the economic aspects of community development (Urban Development Corporations, Task Forces, City Challenge, Single Regeneration Budget), the involvement of the private sector in community regeneration schemes has, not surprisingly, resulted in a similar focus. There is a danger of community development being drawn or skewed into a wholly economic or business framework. Potentially this could have two effects: the strategy of using community work to support community groups in neighbourhoods could be squeezed out, and the scope for injecting community development ideas and experience into social programmes could be lost.

At the same time that the local nature of community development has been challenged by these trends, its central concern with collective action and organisation has had to handle an unprecedented emphasis by government on individualism, consumerism and privatisation.

Community development organisations have sought to cope with these powerful forces in a number of ways. At the policy level, they have taken seriously government encouragement of self-help and voluntary work by putting the case for recognition of the strengths and diversity of the community sector as a distinctive part of the voluntary sector in general (Chanan, 1992). At the same time they have increased their commitment to working in partnership with a wide range of statutory, voluntary and private sector organisations. In addition to helping to promote community development ideas, this approach has had the effect of improving the credibility of community development.

Yet the picture is a bleak one, particularly when viewed through the eyes of local community workers and activists. Mary McAleese (1990), an experienced church community worker in Liverpool who has committed herself to Community Organising, has used the phrase 'shared hope in hopelessness' to describe her response to the pain of many urban communities. In the early 1990s there was little sign of a shared framework or vision to which community workers and others could relate. They were thrown back on their own inner strengths and networks.

Community Organising appeared to offer a coherent alternative to the prevailing all-dominant ideology. It could fill the void which traditional community development was unable to fill. Its message and its methods appeared to offer a way out of the despair in which many community workers felt themselves to be trapped. This point was recognised by Neil Jameson:

> 'I do think that broad-based community organising is a strategy for the 1990s in the UK partly because of the apparent centralisation of political power around Mrs Thatcher, which has served to emphasise the powerlessness millions of people were already feeling in this country. However effective community workers may be locally, they have proved less effective with city/area-wide issues and concerns and any successes have tended to be very short term' (Jameson, 1990).

Community Organising thus offers the possibility of a way forward in a situation where, particularly in the church context, there has been an absence of political action. Could this method of intervention be the spark to ignite a vibrant social justice lobby based not solely on the deliberations of national churches and voluntary organisations but on the voices and actions of local people?

Finding the links

We noted earlier how a succession of individuals in the UK went to the USA to experience training in Community Organising. Their numbers were small, but the individuals concerned were able to make use of their learning on their return. For example, project leaders and middle managers in the South-West and Wales region of the Children's Society played key roles in galvanising others. The courses appear to have been well-run and intensive – and very challenging to the UK visitors. A participant from Liverpool, for example, reported:

> 'There were about 180 on the course…. The IAF training was presented in 19 x 2 hour sessions morning, afternoon and evening. In addition, one evening (after an afternoon briefing), we attended an 'action' organised jointly by the four IAF affiliates in Los Angeles to launch their campaign for better public education – Kids 1st' (Brain, 1990, p. 1).

The strategy of the enthused, on returning to the UK, was to avoid being drawn into a classic national campaigning role. Rather they committed themselves to building constituencies in a limited number of cities and wider areas: 'Community Organising is a long-term strategy for change which requires the slow and painstaking building of a broad power base first, before any issues, local or area-wide, can be tackled' (Jameson, 1990). In 1988, as a first step towards introducing this method of working into the British situation, a number of people set up the Citizen Organising Foundation.

The first initiative was launched in Bristol in 1990. The organiser, Neil Jameson, successfully brought together church leaders, and the inaugural meeting of Communities Organised for a Greater Bristol (COGB) was attended by more than 1,200 people. The Bishop of Bristol commented that the initiative 'has all the possibilities of being the most radical movement with which the churches have engaged in this century'. COGB's stated aims were to bring key institutions – congregations, community and tenants' associations – into a broad-based community organisation. Initial members included Methodist, Pentecostal, Roman Catholic, Hindu and Church of England congregations.

Since then, often with the assistance of grants from the Church Urban Fund, new organisations have been developed in Merseyside, the Black Country, East London, Wales and Sheffield. Fircroft College in Birmingham outlined proposals for an education and training centre for Community Organising. There has been an exchange programme between community workers in Northern Ireland and the USA. One success for Community Organising was the willingness of two trusts, the Barrow Cadbury Trust and the Gulbenkian Foundation, to make grants to help the development of the movement in the UK. This commitment might be seen as symbolising the inter-relationship of the central themes we are exploring: the crisis in Britain's Urban Priority Areas (UPAs), the 'traditions' and potential of indigenous community development (of which trusts such as Cadbury and Gulbenkian have been important supporters) and the experiences of Community Organising in the USA.

Community Organising in the UK is poised between this threeway relationship, and it is this which we shall explore in the next section. Arguably, the key question revolves around applicability. Given its North American origins, given the political and social structure of Britain in the mid-1990s and given the conventional wisdoms of community development in the UK, will Community Organising work?

4 Risks and Potential

Observers of Community Organising in the USA have raised questions about it. What constitutes 'effectiveness'? Can the movement's success or failure be identified? What happens to long-established community organisations? And are democratic structures within community organisations compatible with the personality cult sometimes associated with aspects of Community Organising?

Our starting point is a little different from this wide-ranging treatment in that, having first set out the approach and methods which characterise Community Organising, we propose to examine it specifically in relation to British society and its institutions, and the experiences and assumptions of British community work.

Approach and methods

One of the most evident characteristics of Community Organising is that, instead of organising on a neighbourhood-by-neighbourhood basis or on a theme-by-theme basis, it builds up a city-wide 'people's organisation'. It is in this sense that it forms part of the tradition of social movements in the USA.

In order to be effective, the organisation should ideally involve about 80 groups. Forging trust and common agendas between these is crucial; the manifesto announcing COGB states, 'We believe that the process of problem solving and the active participation of ordinary people is as important as the decisions themselves and that this strengthens and enhances the democratic process.'

The methods of Community Organising which support this approach can be summarised as follows.

Public–private

- There is an emphasis on careful listening in order to identify the issues that threaten individuals, families and their neighbourhoods.
- A strong distinction is made between the public and private areas. Relationships in each of these spheres are of contrasting orders: private relationships are naturally loving and accepting, public ones consciously calculating and dependent on self-interest.
- Organisation is 'a series of relationships with a purpose' and meetings to create 'public' relationships are mostly carried out one-to-one and deliberately aim to target powerful individuals and convince them of an argument or the salience of an issue. The one-to-one basis of organising has been described as

16

the most radical feature of IAF. It appeals to the self-interest of potential supporters and participants, and of those holding power.

- Community Organising seeks to turn a problem into an issue, because an issue is specific, immediate and winnable.

Methods

- Being able to mobilise large numbers of people to press for action characterises Community Organising. This is where the alternative term by which the movement is known – Broad-based Organising – is significant. Unlike neighbourhood-based action groups, members of Community Organising can draw on a wide constituency which is based on more than one issue.
- Professional organisers play a central role. They are accountable to the member organisations who work alongside the recognised leaders of religious groups. The latter must have qualities – a strong ego, anger, imagination, humour, honesty – strongly reminiscent of Alinsky's recommendations in *Rules for Radicals* (1972). They hold their leadership positions for limited periods of time. Training of both professional organisers and recognised leaders is seen to be of major importance.
- The main tactic is confrontational, based on careful calculations of what can be gained from any situation – the language of deals. Community Organising concentrates on a single issue at any one time because it is tangible and can be seen to be more winnable than carrying a long agenda of issues.
- Emphasis is put on careful planning and rehearsal before an action. This includes details about handling the press, how visiting speakers will be greeted and heard and what happens if they try to provoke the meeting.
- Evaluation of action taken is given high priority by Community Organising. The purpose is to ensure that the organisation learns from campaigns and activities undertaken so that it can become more effective.

Organisation

- Membership dues are levied on constituent communities and not individual members. Grants are obtained from churches and trusts, but are not sought from local or central government.
- Community Organising is aligned with struggles for social justice. It is not focused on welfare or service delivery. It realises that successes have to be achieved if people are to stay involved. In the same vein, it is aware of the need for fun to be built into actions; long, boring meetings are to be avoided.
- Community Organising favours flexible structures and seeks to avoid any one group coming to dominate the organisation. Similarly, it does not adopt fixed positions with institutions and agencies.

These points outline the main elements of Community Organising. Perhaps the key to all of them is discipline and accountability and the seriousness with which these are taken:

> 'What is promised must be delivered and the strength of the organisation lies in holding people to their word, not allowing them to go off at a tangent on a personal whim. All who join agree to be accountable and that anything done in the name of the group shall be subject to the critique' (Merseyside Churches' Urban Institute, 1991).

The leaders and organisers are accountable to the movement, members are accountable for their actions and – equally important – public figures can always be held to account for their policies and decisions.

What this summary cannot do is convey the extent of the commitment and enthusiasm of those people who are involved in Community Organising: its rootedness in faith and values, its experiences of mobilising large numbers of people around specific issues in Bristol, Merseyside and elsewhere.

Community Organising in the UK context

Those people involved in developing Community Organising in the UK are aware that the American models have to be adjusted. James Pitt and Maurice Keane (1984) made this point in their original report and Neil Jameson has said, 'We do not underestimate the danger of translating US experience – church or secular – wholesale to the UK' (Jameson, 1988). We suggest that there are three key contextual areas which, in the mid-1990s, Community Organising in the UK has to address:

- society and social class,
- politics, and
- the churches.

Society and social class

British observers of American society, in labelling it as dominated by individualism, often miss the point that being a concerned, active citizen is widely commended. In this sense Community Organising taps into a well-worn groove associated strongly with the self-help ethic. Organising at the level of the block where one lives is very common.

One analysis of British society is that the centrality of the welfare state to people's lives has meant there has been less need for the mobilisation of active citizens. Certainly the existence in the UK of welfare institutions and services, however much they may have been eroded over the last 15 years, contrasts significantly with the situation in the USA. A criticism of community action in Britain's cities is that on the whole it has been too inward-looking and parochial. It has only rarely made connections with the poverty lobbies at national and European levels.

The main tradition of community work in Britain has been to intervene in neighbourhoods precisely in order to reaffirm or discover the connections between people by helping them form and strengthen local groups. Community workers have been happy to use the argument that participation is skewed: the heritage of charitable and voluntary organisations, manifested by national membership organisations and voluntary agencies staffed by professionals, is an essentially middle-class one. Supporting the community involvement of working-class people, especially those experiencing long-term unemployment and a poor environment, requires skill and resources. Hence the tradition of placing a community worker, sometimes a small team, on a council estate or in an inner-city area. Hence too the growing evidence indicating that before enterprise agencies can expect successful community business they must ensure that a reasonably strong infrastructure of community groups is in place.

The effect of Conservative social policies has been to reinforce this argument in the sense that inequalities within society, including those areas which have received targeted government interventions, have become more evident. There are large groups of people who are living at or below the poverty line, who are long-term unemployed and/or who are homeless. They may be noticed by the rest of society through statistics, the media or because they are on the streets of city centres, but the impact of destitution is predominantly felt in neighbourhoods. The combination of drug misuse, gangs, nascent violence, fear of crime and other forms of anti-social behaviour in some neighbourhoods makes it very difficult for community development to take place. In these areas community workers will be forced to operate in a social environment characterised by diversity and confusion. Much of their time will be spent in clarifying the current strengths and weaknesses of groups, in helping groups to keep going and to support the formation of new groups.

In depicting communities and community work in this way, we are aware that we risk caricaturing the UK situation. Our concern, however, is to ask questions about the points of fusion or contact between Community Organising and local communities. The chemistry of the interaction between the two will be a critical determinant of Community Organising's chances of success. It opens up questions about leadership in communities; in particular how 'ascribed' leaders, people whose authority derives from their organisational or political position, are regarded by local people. Is the basis of the relationship essentially one of deference or does it have the potential to be a relationship of equals?

Questions about community and leadership need to be posed alongside a strong awareness of the cultural differences which exist within the UK, especially those based on feelings of national or ethnic identity. As Alan Evans points out when discussing the potential of Community Organising in Wales, there has to be 'an authentic response to Welsh concerns with strategies appropriate for this situation' (Evans, 1988).

In the USA, many activists in 'communities of colour' have built groups outside the mainstream of Community Organising because it was seen as taking insufficient account of race (Delgado, 1994). Given the links in the UK between community action and religious and ethnic loyalties, it will be essential for Community Organising to take seriously the cultural identities of communities. Ethnic groups will often not see the relevance of geographical definitions of 'community'. They 'form and mobilise around the push for maintenance (in some cases re-creation) of ethnic heritage, and the search for an "essential ethnicity" to which they can lay claim' (Meekosha, 1993, p. 186).

Electoral politics

It is only comparatively recently that some streams of North American Community Organising have sought to work within the framework of the electoral political system; traditionally the movement has seen itself as providing a way of challenging that system. Local managers and other political leaders have often been the main targets of actions. A similar strain of community action has been very important, historically, in the UK. Indeed, much of the anger and energy of local people springs from a strong sense of disillusion with the traditional political system – broken promises, inability to listen to local voices, the perceived inflexibility of the system.

The picture in the mid-1990s, however, has changed radically since the late 1960s when spontaneous local action was so much in evidence. On the one hand, for reasons touched on earlier, expressions of campaigning community action have declined. Exhaustion, realisation of the hurdles that have to be cleared, the need to put energy into personal and group survival strategies, the resource implications of organising across a city, let alone nationally – all of these begin to explain why the decline has taken place.

At the same time the professional or occupational stream of community development has increasingly seen the need to operate at the level of policy as well as practice. Perhaps criticisms made of community workers over the years that they were being drawn into a cul-de-sac of localism were listened to: neighbourhood action was necessary but not sufficient. Certainly during the 1980s there was a greater willingness to acknowledge the limitation, as far as social change was concerned, of practice operating on its own. The Association of Metropolitan Authorities (AMA) reports on community development (AMA, 1989, 1993), and the contribution of community development to local authority anti-poverty strategies, both illustrate the shift to policy working. It was community workers positioned inside local authorities who could play a lead role here. Not only were they themselves employed within the electoral system, they also argued that local authority elected members and staff have crucial parts to play in supporting and promoting community development.

Both of the above trends – the weakening of community action, the growth of community development policy and strategy work – suggest the relationship of Community Organising to electoral politics in the UK needs careful analysis.

A different but equally important line of enquiry is about political decision-making in the UK. There is increasing evidence that this has become much more centralised in recent years. Central government funding for local authorities has decreased significantly, and the funds which are available are tightly controlled by Whitehall. How does this major change affect the approach of Community Organising, given its concern with local issues and targeting of local leaders?

Churches

The differences between churches in the USA and those in the UK have been noted by several commentators on Community Organising – the stronger tradition of the American parish, the high level of attendance at American churches, the relative weaknesses of British churches in disadvantaged neighbourhoods, the question of whether there may be limitations in the main church involved in Community Organising being the 'established' church, and a query about the strength of ecumenism: will groups come together across denominations?

Advocates of Community Organising will argue – with some justification – that those problems are surmountable. There have been clashes between grassroots church workers and church leaders in Bristol. However, Jay MacLeod contends that Community Organising will be a challenge to the paternalism of British churches and that it also holds the promise of new hope for urban congregations. This optimism has still to be tested. More questionable is his statement that Community Organising is 'a powerful vehicle for inter-faith and inter-denominational ecumenism' (MacLeod, 1993, p. 13). Can Community Organising really claim to be genuinely broad-based, knitting together allies not only across the Christian denominations but also across other churches and religions, agnostics and atheists? Can an organisation be both broad-based and church-based? And can we expect Muslims and members of other faiths to form part of Community Organising on the same basis as Christian churches are involved?

Community Organising – strengths and dangers

There are a number of features of Community Organising which make its potential as a force for social change in the UK considerable. There are also risks associated with it. We offer some broader reflections on these questions in the final section. Here we list those points which, given the approach of Community Organising and the UK context outlined here, seem to us to be areas that have most potential and risks.

Potential

- Linking neighbourhood-based organisations across a town or city around issues perceived to be important by people can be extremely effective.
- Planning and preparing actions with the assumption that they are winnable can be a strength – as can being open about the realities of power.
- Realisation of the importance of training leaders and of rehearsing tactics could be critical in reawakening hope and bringing success to communities.
- Building in clear lines of accountability of leaders to their stated tasks and membership could make demands of communities clearer, more incisive.
- The emphasis on evaluation and on learning from actions can be a key asset.
- Clarity about which sources of funding provide most scope for social justice struggles can bring success and underline the value of autonomy.

Risks

- Is Community Organising so concerned with building issue-based alliances and with focusing on winnable issues that it will not respond to the particular needs or demands of minority groups, such as people with disabilities or children?
- The confrontational style of Community Organising has a 'macho' element which may appear strange or alien to some community groups.
- There is a risk that Community Organising, in its eagerness to develop a power analysis, will over-personalise situations, thereby undermining belief in the value of all people.
- Alinsky was committed to democracy but he sometimes operated in a non-democratic way. His directiveness was often associated with manipulation. Community Organising will need to be alert to this danger.
- There may be a question of groups being over-dependent on the organiser, for Community Organisations appear to require long-term support. Woodlawn in Chicago, for example, ran into trouble when the organiser was withdrawn.
- An emphasis on self-interest as the key to organising risks reducing community involvement to narrow or materialistic concerns. It can also exacerbate divisions in communities, setting one group against another:

'Community Organising seems to equate justice with getting a bit more of the 'cake' for me/my community within a context in which every problem can be dealt with. It demands no real change in individual attitudes, no understanding of wider political or moral agendas, no sense of interdependence outside the organisation/community' (Martin, 1990).

5 State of the Art?

Having identified aspects of Community Organising which suggest it has much to offer communities and community development in Britain, and those traits against which there are question marks, we now set the scene for a dialogue between Community Organising and community development.

There is a considerable body of literature available in the UK dealing with community development. So far, however, little has been written about Community Organising, and most of what has been written is partisan. Authors have either been strongly committed to the movement as a form of intervention, or else equally strongly opposed to it. In this section, we seek to offer a more neutral assessment in the hope that it will contribute to a constructive debate, in which Community Organising might be looked at in a broader context. The concluding section contains a summary of future possibilities, and an indication of some of the issues which could usefully form the basis for a discussion between exponents of Community Organising and those who practise more traditional forms of community work.

Because Community Organising is church led, and because it has been established in the UK since the publication of *Faith in the City* (1985), it is inevitably seen as a partial response to the Archbishop of Canterbury's Commission's challenge to the churches to become more active in community work in Urban Priority Areas. This linkage is reinforced by the fact that those applying to the Church Urban Fund for financial support for Community Organising draw upon the recommendations in *Faith in the City* in their submissions.

The emphasis of Community Organising on issues of justice and the empowerment of the powerless is clearly compatible with the general aims of the CUF. Since the Fund was created, the Trustees have financed a large number of community-based initiatives in UPAs which would claim to have similar priorities. The differences between Community Organising and most of the other projects supported by the CUF are mainly to do with scale, methods, objectives and style.

Two preliminary points need to be made. The first is that though Community Organising draws upon many years of experience in the USA, it is still at a very early stage of development in this country. Communities Organised for a Greater Bristol (COGB) was launched in 1990 and Merseyside Broad-Based Organising (MBO) only in 1993. Other initiatives in East London, Sheffield and the Black Country are still in the process of being established. Community Organising is conceived as a long-term movement rather than a short-term project, and this is one of its virtues. There is a recognition that the three-to-five year life-span of so many community-based projects is wholly inadequate for achieving significant social change.

The second point to be emphasised is that there is no doubt about the commitment, vision and integrity of those who have set up the Citizen Organising Foundation and have subsequently made Community Organising a reality. Some of the people, who in the mid-1980s visited the USA to look at the work of the IAF, had wide experience of different forms of community practice in this country. They were acutely aware of how little had been achieved by numerous community-based projects and government-led initiatives. People in UPAs remained largely powerless, and on most indices their conditions were relatively worse than they had been at the end of the 1960s. After 1979 the ideological climate changed. Collectivism was under attack and the virtues of individualism were constantly extolled. Through their encounters with advocates and practitioners of Community Organising, some of those who travelled to America felt that they had discovered a way forward, and they have worked long and hard to translate their American experience into a form of organising which they believe to be appropriate for the UK.

Community work

What scope is there within the experience and occupation of British community work for lodging Community Organising more firmly within communities and the intervention activities of community workers? The paper by Joe Hasler (1990), in which he questions the appeal to self-interest, the emphasis on winnable actions and the strong distinction made between public and private worlds, was published initially as a discussion paper by the then British Council of Churches (BCC). It is a strongly written document in which the author sets out 'to question … the exclusive use of Alinsky's methods for Church related community workers given the nature of the church's value base'. It provoked a strong response from Dave Berry, who in the BCC's newsletter registered his concern at the 'appalling lack of professionalism' in British community/youth work: 'If community workers are not able to grasp a vision based on action, then I fear for the future of community work in the UK' (Berry, 1990).

Our own discussion of Community Organising seeks to unravel the points that were raised by Hasler and Berry. We are concerned to encourage a discussion which did not happen as a result of the exchange between two experienced community workers. One explanation for the absence of debate is the reluctance of those committed to Community Organising to engage in such activities. Their training does not encourage this; debate is perceived either as being a lower priority compared with setting up and supporting Community Organising or as being diversionary. Leaving aside, for the moment, questions relating to the value basis of Community Organising and reflecting specifically on how it relates to community work as an intervention, we would make the following three points.

Practice-theory

At one level, the tenets of Community Organising are reminiscent of the maxim coined by Jim Radford (1978): 'Don't agonise, organise.' Yet this appeal to community workers to trust their instincts when supporting local action did not seek to deny the existence and importance of good practice. It was warning community workers against becoming dominated by academia, not an argument against thinking carefully about what community workers do and how they work with local people.

Within community work, there has been a consistent interest in methods over the last 20 years. Good-quality guides on the nuts and bolts of how community groups can be most effective have been published at regular intervals, while generalist textbooks on the 'how to do it' aspects are used on community work, social work and other basic training courses.

Community Organising shares the concern with the detail of organising; indeed it can be argued that it is attention to detail which does much to account for the movement's track record of mobilising and organising large numbers of people. Our point is that this seam of Community Organising's experience needs to compare notes with the equivalent British community work experience.

The importance of the knowledge and skills which have been built up by community work should not be underestimated. They mean that community workers can speak with authority about the difficulties involved in initiating and supporting local action, and of the methods and techniques which have been shown to be most effective. Is Community Organising going to relate to this practice-theory?

Role

The community worker's role when supporting local people has been of continuing interest to community workers, trainers and writers. Often the discussion has focused on the question of the extent to which community workers should be directive or non-directive. It has also pinpointed issues to do with the values of workers: how far they should reveal beliefs and commitments when facilitating a group.

It is difficult to know whether or not Community Organising would give priority to these concerns. What one can say is that organisers fit within the directive category and, compared with their directive counterparts in the UK, they would be much more demanding of local leaders – keeping them at the task, insisting on evaluating actions, reminding them of accountability: 'Rather like a good teacher [the organiser's] job is to challenge the leader and to spur him or her on to do better work. The relationship should not be too cosy'(Twelvetrees, 1988).

At the same time Community Organising is very clear that leaders and organisers do not usurp the decision-making process. Possibly to a greater degree than their British counterparts, they are careful to remind members that this is their responsibility.

Participation

A key question for the UK community worker has been to do with the openness of groups: how possible is it for people lacking experience and self-confidence, or who belong to a minority group, to become involved? It is relatively easy for a community worker to relate to existing patterns of participation in neighbourhoods; much more challenging is to encourage the involvement of the powerless and excluded. This is where the community worker's skills are tested most severely. Usually it requires a combination of patience and perseverance by the worker, essentially an educative approach over a long-term period.

Is this strand of British community work seen to be important by Community Organising, or does its concern with mobilising large numbers of people around a single winnable issue mean that this aspect of participation has low priority? One of the strongest arguments for investing in community work is that, primarily because of its values, it offers the possibility of enabling poor, disadvantaged communities to have a voice – less the cry of despair of the individual, more the public demands of people acting together. Arguably, encouraging such opportunities, and witnessing the changes in both individuals and groups, can be as important as winning on an issue.

Planning and power

Turning from community work to Community Organising, many of its strengths can be traced back to its American track record. Meetings, at every level, are well planned, crisp and purposeful. Common self-interests are reduced to clearly defined winnable issues around which action can be taken. Whereas community development is concerned with process and workers are reluctant to be directive, Community Organising is about building an organisation which can act effectively, and the lead organiser operates accordingly.

Community Organising emphasises the importance of power. The aim is to build an organisation capable of exercising power. This means that it must be both broad in its composition and large in terms of the number of people who can be involved in campaigns. The contrast with the small-scale projects of community action with which we are familiar in the UK is all too clear.

A power analysis is carried out in relation to specific issues. The objective is to identify the person who has the power to do something about the issue being tackled. This person then becomes the target of action by the organisation. We have seen this process played out by the COGB when, in respect of two separate issues, the Chair of Bristol West Building Society and the Chief Constable of Avon have respectively been identified as the people holding power and have therefore been selected as targets for action. This willingness to take power seriously is one of the strengths of Community Organising.

Community Organising has always been strong on tactics, and has never been afraid to engage in confrontation. In the UK there has been a reluctance to employ confrontational tactics, and this has been particularly true of Christians. It is refreshing, therefore, to see what is predominantly a church-based organisation accepting that there are times when the quest for social justice can involve conflicts of interests – whether or not this justifies confrontational tactics is another matter.

Community Organising has a commendable singleness of purpose. It is concerned with campaigning, not service provision. Unlike most of the other projects which are financed through the CUF, Community Organising does not engage in 'ambulance' work or self-help. Instead, it concentrates on creating a new power base so that people can take action on issues which affect their common interests.

Money and members

In his earliest days as an organiser, Alinsky saw the importance of independent funding for any organisation committed to empowering the powerless. From the beginning, Community Organising has taken this principle on board. IAF-based Community Organising seeks no funds from government sources and does not solicit money from vested interests. This is clearly one of its strengths.

Over a three-year period, CUF gave grants totalling £60,000 to COGB and MBO. The remainder of their income comes from other trust funds and fees from member groups. They seek eventually to become self-funding through monies levied from constituent groups, but in the medium term they are likely to remain dependent upon supplementary funding from a variety of sources.

At this stage in the development of Community Organising, success can be measured mainly in terms of organisation-building in Bristol and on Merseyside. In both areas, large organisations have been created in a comparatively short period of time. By January 1994, COGB consisted of 26 member communities and MBO of 41. Though the organisations are mainly composed of church communities, there are also some communities drawn from other faiths as well as a few non-religious groups. Both COGB and MBO have a wide social mix, and it is evident that many participants have gained from a sense of solidarity.

Even allowing for some exaggeration in the claims about the number of people directly and indirectly involved in the two organisations, the response remains impressive when compared with the numbers belonging to other community and political groupings over comparable geographical areas.

It is difficult to judge the degree of effectiveness of the actions which have so far been undertaken. The causal connection between action and eventual policy changes is not always easy to establish. COGB has tended to act on broad issues, like homelessness and local government reorganisation, as well as on more localised issues, such as the provision of bus shelters and traffic calming, whereas MBO, which was launched later than COGB, has so far concentrated on local issues like road safety and fly-tipping. However, in both areas many people in positions of responsibility are now aware of the presence of organisations capable of mounting carefully planned and sustained action on clearly defined issues.

In assessing Community Organising, we recognise the limitations of more traditional forms of community practice. Achievements have often been modest, and in some instances merely cosmetic. Many of the other community projects funded by the CUF have made little impact on the inequalities referred to in *Faith in the City* (1985) and the problems currently experienced in UPAs. We can, therefore, understand the frustration of those who have looked across the Atlantic for a more effective way of empowering people and improving their conditions. Like them, we hope that Community Organising will prove more successful than earlier initiatives. However, our experience and enquiries still cause us to have a number of reservations. These are briefly outlined below.

Exclusion?

Reference was made earlier to the undoubted commitment, integrity and vision of those who succeeded in setting up the COF and getting Community Organising off the ground. Unfortunately, visionaries can be so single-minded that they begin to exclude those who do not share their vision. Certainly there are people who *feel* that they were excluded as soon as they started to raise doubts and questions about Community Organising. This impression has been strengthened by the reluctance of key people to enter into discussions about their approach. The explanation offered has been that the need is to engage in action rather than dialogue.

An ethos has developed around Community Organising which is not conducive to open debate, and which some people experience as being intimidating. Enthusiasts have become 'precious' about Community Organising, and their intensity has made people on the fringe feel uncomfortable. This is alien to the spirit of more traditional community work, which has been open, non-secretive and relaxed.

In the USA, Community Organising developed a style which has – to some extent – been carried over to the UK. It tended to be very macho, and it was a long time before women became organisers. The emphasis upon confrontation has reinforced this image. Though a woman was appointed as one of the first two lead organisers in the UK, there is still a strong male influence in Community Organising. No doubt the organisers are sensitive to the gender issue, but given the prominent role played by clergy and priests – predominantly male – it will not be easy to redress the imbalance. The trustees of COF are six white male leaders from the churches. As women are over-represented amongst the most oppressed sections of society, the style and the leadership roles within Community Organising are of more than symbolic importance.

This leads to another reservation about the movement. It has what appears to be a very formal democratic structure, and yet in the way it operates it appears to favour authoritarian methods which we believe do not sit easily with democratic values. We are thinking especially of its targeting or 'pinning' approach to individuals.

A related point concerns the nature of membership. One of the criticisms of COGB is that, because its membership is based more on middle-class communities than on Urban Priority Areas, this has had an undue influence on policy and the selection of issues. In contrast, MBO draws most of its membership communities from UPAs. In both organisations religious leaders are influential. The tendency is to identify people who have already shown leadership skills, whereas in many CUF projects the emphasis is on enabling new people to develop these skills.

Churches only?

There is also an apparent contradiction between the description 'broad-based' and the practice of making churches the main building blocks of the organisations. This again can be traced back to the earliest days of American Community Organising, when a Judaeo-Christian value base was adopted. In the UK there has been a widening out to include 'other' faiths and some non-religious groups. However, the composition of the first two British Community Organisations is so heavily weighted towards the churches that it is not easy for secular and other-faith groups to feel that they are in an equal partnership.

It was probably tactically unwise to begin by concentrating on recruiting Christian congregations as members. Indeed, given the financial and numerical weakness of the British churches and the importance of minority ethnic organisations in most of our urban areas, it might have been better to have operated from the beginning on the basis of a much wider constituency. Even from a Christian perspective, COGB and MBO are not fully ecumenical. In Bristol it is predominantly Anglican churches which are involved, while on Merseyside Catholic churches are in a large majority with apparently no participation by Free Churches. In both areas, minority ethnic groups are under-represented, and in Bristol there seems to have been little success in involving the city's black churches.

A declared objective of Community Organising is empowerment, but the work carried out so far in Greater Bristol and on Merseyside raises questions about who is being empowered. Reference has already been made to a possible imbalance between middle-class and UPA involvement in Bristol, and to the way that in both areas existing leaders often take on leadership roles within CO. No doubt some residents from deprived areas will feel empowered through their participation in a large citizen-based organisation, but our impression is that Community Organising has so far been comparatively unsuccessful in empowering the most powerless. This can be largely attributed to the way it goes about creating a new organisation, and the geographical scale on which it operates.

By using the churches as the main building blocks, vast numbers of poor, marginalised and powerless people are excluded. Except in predominantly Catholic areas, very few of them belong to the churches, or to any other formal group. By working primarily with religious institutions, Community Organising fails to get through to the least-strong members of society. Its intervention is pitched at a level above that where most powerless people are to be found.

Power analysis

The empowerment of the most powerless is further hindered by involving religious congregations from such large geographical areas. Inevitably, they are socially, ethnically and economically diverse, and are linked only by a vague, conceptual statement about values. With such a wide spread, it is predictable that decision-making and leadership will not be exercised by the most powerless people. Community development with its tradition of working in poor neighbourhoods compares more favourably with Community Organising in relation to empower-ment, as it generates a sense of solidarity between people in similar circumstances and enables them to take control of their own groups. If we are to look to America for ideas, then ACORN's emphasis on building an organisation through the intensive recruitment of individuals is arguably more likely to lead to empowerment and autonomy.

Earlier in this section, Community Organising's emphasis on power was picked out as one of its strengths, but a caveat must be added to this. In stressing the importance of power, advocates of Community Organising are close to Saul Alinsky. However, his analysis was limited. He did not relate his work to the wider political and structural context of American society. Tactics consisted largely of taking action against accessible local power-holders – civic leaders, landlords, captains of industry, board members of institutions. Though key people in Community Organising are clearly aware of the national and international dimensions of power, this is not reflected in what happens on the ground.

To focus on individuals who are identified as exercising power is to underesti-mate the extent to which they themselves are constrained by the systems within which they function. Even the campaign by COGB directed at forcing Bristol West Building Society to provide social housing does not get anywhere near tackling the housing crisis, created by more than a decade of underfunding accompanied by policies which have driven young people on to the streets. In its practice, Community Organising largely ignores the ideological and structural nature of inequalities in our society, and – like a lot of community work – spends much of its time taking up real, but secondary, issues.

There are important contextual differences between the USA and the UK in the way that power is distributed and exercised. Even during the period when the right has been dominant in both countries, there has been a major difference between the policies of the respective governments in relation to local democracy. Whereas in the UK there have been 40 Acts of Parliament since 1979 regulating local government, in the USA there has been a lifting of restrictions in order to strengthen local accountability. In 1981 the Reagan administration did away with numerous limitations on how local and state authorities could use federal funds. Both governments have, however, created an ethos in which low taxes and low public expenditure are regarded as prime virtues.

Whereas local government functions in the UK in a similar way across England, Scotland and Wales, in North America it varies immensely from area to area. Generally, the system is much more fragmented, and there are more points at which some power is exercised.

These are factors which affect community organisations' scope for action. The contextual differences have important implications for Community Organising, and the founding members of COF and the lead organisers clearly appreciate the need for adaptation, as is indicated by the widening of their value base to include people from faiths outside the Judaeo-Christian tradition. However, it is unlikely that this understanding is widely shared and that sufficient account is taken of political, cultural, social and religious differences.

A caveat must also be added to our praise for the principle of independent funding. How realistic it is in practice is open to question. At the moment, both COGB and MBO are heavily dependent upon the CUF and other trusts, and financial projections for the future do not suggest that membership fees from constituent groups will match expenditure. If – as in the case with ACORN – membership was on an individual basis, with each member contributing on a monthly or annual basis, then there would be a way of determining the level of personal commitment and – possibly – of achieving self-funding.

6 The Future?

In the USA, IAF-type Community Organising has been practised for well over 50 years. There have been changes, but its basic aims and methods have remained the same. What are the prospects for the British version?

It could continue to develop in isolation from other forms of community practice. This will mean that tension between Community Organising and more traditional community work would continue. There would be further misunderstandings about goals, methods and styles of operating, and sometimes these would create confusion for congregations and communities.

An optimistic view would be that separate development could lead to Community Organising being adopted in more and more urban areas, with opportunities opening up for co-operation and common action between organisations. On the other hand, it could – like many other well-intentioned radical initiatives – prove unsustainable on anything other than a short-term basis.

An alternative scenario is possible, however. It is that community practitioners who share a common commitment to empowerment and social justice should begin to develop complementary strategies for achieving their goals. There are a number of key problems which have never been solved by traditional forms of community work, and which on the record of North American experience are unlikely to be solved by the UK version of Community Organising. However, both traditions have contributions to make to finding a solution. An eclectic approach needs to be adopted, with a willingness on the part of everyone to be open and receptive to a wide range of ideas and experience.

The problems have been alluded to earlier, but for clarity they are set out in this concluding section.

Probably the key issue confronting community work practitioners is how to match the action to the analysis. Bodies such as the Association of Community Workers, the Federation of Community Work Training Groups and the Standing Conference for Community Development have consistently held to a structural rather than pathological explanation of the causes of inequality, and the vast majority of community workers would share this view. Much of the practice does not match the analysis. Practitioners are trapped into responding to crises, and into working with people on palliatives rather than solutions.

Community Organising is partly a response to this failure on the part of traditional community work. It does not simply respond to the latest crisis, and it refuses to become involved in service provision. However, so far there is little evidence that it is being much more successful than community work in bringing about significant changes. A criticism of IAF is that over its long history, it has failed to change or modify the structures in the USA which are increasing the level of poverty.

Both traditional community work and Community Organising are committed to the mobilisation of poor people in order to bring about change. They need to explore how this can be done in a way which is compatible with their analysis.

A related problem has to do with the process of centralisation and the growth of unaccountable bodies. Local authorities have seen their powers progressively eroded, and this applies particularly to their capacity to raise money. This has had serious consequences for community work. Neighbourhood campaigns to attract additional services or resources now have little chance of success because of the cash limits imposed by central government. Any success gained is likely to be at the expense of a similar low-income area. An additional difficulty is that some services are now controlled by unaccountable quangos.

In the USA, where power is generally more decentralised, the situation has also changed. Delgado (1994) comments that changes in government spending policies have had 'a chilling effect on CO's ability to deliver "wins" to local communities'. He adds that in the present complex political decision-making arena, 'consolidated geographic neighbourhood organisations' are less effective than they used to be. If we are to learn from North America, then we need to note such observations and relate them to our own experience.

Changes have taken place in the last few years which affect both Community Organising and traditional community work. Those involved in the process of empowerment should discuss the implications of these changes for practice.

We have already commented on the way that in the USA Community Organising has tended to move up-market, leaving the poorest neighbourhoods unorganised. Of course there are arguments for this. Stable working- and middle-class communities are easier to organise, middle-class people exercise more influence, and organisations based on existing institutional groups are likely to have greater social cohesion. There is a similar problem in the UK, though it tends to be less obvious. Traditional community work sometimes draws heavily upon local professionals, and even when it does not do this it can unwittingly engage in a 'creaming off' process which results in unrepresentative groups.

Community Organising has a particular problem in this respect. It is an inevitable consequence of being predominantly based upon an institution which has little influence in the most deprived urban areas. For religious and cultural reasons this is more of a problem for COGB than for MBO.

This is not an issue over which to score points in a debate, but something that needs to be dealt with constructively.

There is another aspect to this problem which is more apparent in the USA than it is in the UK. It has to do with the relative failure of Community Organising to respond to race and gender issues. According to Delgado, even as late as 1985 there were few women or 'people of colour' in positions of authority in US community organisations. In Britain community work took these issues on board at a much earlier stage in its development. The Association of Community Workers, for instance, started to deal with the problem of male–white bias in its own organisation in the mid-1970s, but we have no grounds for being satisfied with the broad picture.

In the USA, the vacuum left by Community Organising's structures has been filled by an increasing number of organisations based upon ethnic identity. There are ghettos where black people are beginning to assert control over their own neighbourhoods. In the UK the demography is different, and there are multiracial areas where the mix of the population is at least partly reflected in the composition of community groups. But again there is little room for satisfaction.

Because black people are over-represented in groups of unemployed and low-paid people, any tendency to drift away from working with the poorest sections of the population will exacerbate the under-representation of people from minority ethnic groups in community organisations.

What was said above about Community Organising applies equally to this aspect of the problem. The church-led nature of the movement compounds the difficulties associated with creating organisations which can represent issues of gender, race and sexual orientation as well as issues based on class.

Both Community Organising and those who represent the interests of traditional forms of community work need to give consideration to questions related to the politics of identity.

A problem which is certainly shared by both traditional community work and the new approach is that of funding. Even in America, where private foundations and progressive religious bodies have dispensed vast sums of money, Community Organising is finding it increasingly difficult to obtain resources. In the UK the funding of community projects and community workers has always been precarious. Now the position is acute. For the Church Urban Fund there is a particular dilemma. How should it apportion its modest funds between Community Organising and other types of church-based community projects?

Community work initiatives are constantly having to compete for scarce resources. Searching for funds is time-consuming and saps morale. Many projects have to compromise their independence and freedom of action by trying to respond to the conditions attached to the government's latest pot of money. Now it is the Single Regeneration Budget. Not long ago it was the City Challenge lottery.

Community Organising is right in principle in its commitment to independent funding. But the question which arises is: is it viable?

This is a problem of a different kind from others which have been summarised, but it is a shared issue that needs to be discussed. How can funds be raised for the purpose of sustaining radical initiatives aimed at empowering people and promoting social justice?

Earlier we said that one of the aims of this booklet is to promote a debate between those who represent different approaches to working with people to achieve change. In this final section, we have set out an agenda of some of the issues which need to be considered. They do not represent a flight into theoretical reflection, but are problems arising from practice. We have tried to show that they are not just problems for Community Organising, but also for more traditional forms of community work.

There is general agreement between those who work in inner-city areas and on blighted estates that the situation is serious. Inequalities are growing, alienation is deepening and there is a strong distrust of politicians. Most practitioners recognise that they are making little or no impact on the structures which shape people's lives. If empowering the powerless is to be more than a slogan, then it is essential that we build on our experience, share our insights and learn from others.

We need an eclectic approach whereby we unashamedly borrow from many sources. The methods of ACORN and Citizen Action should be put alongside those of the IAF. But we need to extend our net even further. What can we learn about the way labour has organised itself in the workplace? Alinsky derived his inspiration from the methods Herb March and his trade union colleagues used in organising the packing workers in Chicago. What can we learn from the women's movement? And from the way the African National Congress organised people in the townships of South Africa? If we are thinking about the role of the churches, what about the influence exercised by the Moral Majority in the USA? This movement has refined lobbying into a fine art. Is it not possible for progressive people in the churches to adopt a similar strategy? What back-up can research provide?

It is impossible to predict the outcome of the kind of dialogue which is being advocated, but it is hoped that solutions will be found to some of the problems identified. There could be a recognition of the need to work with different kinds of constituencies and at different levels – neighbourhood, interest group, city, regional and national – and also of the need for a shared vision of social justice. It would help if groups and organisations developed complementary strategies.

In the USA it has been found that 'intermediary bodies' such as training agencies, groups of consultants and researchers have been able to promote some of the most progressive initiatives. In the UK there are few such agencies, but probably the kind of constructive debate that is envisaged could take place under the auspices of a body like the Standing Conference for Community Development. This booklet's contribution to such an exchange has been to suggest some of the topics for the agenda.

References

Alinsky, Saul (1972) *Rules for Radicals* (New York: Vintage Books)

Archbishop of Canterbury's Commission on Urban Priority Areas (1985) *Faith in the City* (London: Church House Publishing)

Association of Metropolitan Authorities (1989) *Community Development – the Local Authority Role* (London: AMA)

Association of Metropolitan Authorities (1993) *Local Authorities and Community Development: A Strategic Opportunity for the 1990s* (London: AMA)

Austin, J. (1989) 'Some Challenges to the Church Arising from Community Development' in *Changing the Agenda* (London: British Council of Churches), pp. 57–69.

Berry, D. (1990) 'On Community Organising' in *Newsletter, Community Work Resource Unit*, British Council of Churches, summer 1990

Boyte, Harry C. (1984) *Community is Possible: Repairing American Roots* (New York: Harper & Row)

Brain, P. (1990) edited extract of a report on the ten-day basic training course run by IAF in Los Angeles, July 1990, mimeo, p. 1.

Chanan, G. (1992) *Out of the Shadows* (Dublin: European Foundation for the Improvement of Living and Working Conditions)

Delgado, G. (1986) *Organising the Movement: The Roots and Growth of ACORN* (Temple University Press)

Delgado, G. (1994) *Beyond the Politics of Place: New Directions in Community Organizing in the 1990s* (Oakland, CA: Applied Research Centre)

Evans, A. (1988) 'Community Organising in Wales in the 1980s' in *Christian Action Journal*, autumn, pp. 1–11

Farnell, R., Lund, S., Furbey, R., Lawless P., Wishart, B. and Else, P. (1994) *Broad-based Organising: An Evaluation for the Church Urban Fund* (Sheffield: Centre for Regional Economic and Social Research, Sheffield Hallam University)

Hasler, J. (1990) 'Community Organising – An Offer You Might Refuse' in ed. P. Ballard, *Issues in Church Related Community Work* (Cardiff: University of Cardiff), pp. 99–102 (first published in *Issues in Church Related Community Work* no. 17, British Council of Churches)

Kenrick, B. (1962) *Come out of the Wilderness* (London: Collins)

Jameson, N. (1988) 'Organising for a Change', editorial in *Christian Action Journal* autumn (London: Christian Action), pp. 4–5

Jameson, N. (1990) personal communication

McAleese, M. (1990) 'Charity, Hope and Faith' in ed. P. Ballard, *Issues in Church Related Community Work*, (Cardiff: University of Cardiff), pp. 80–84

MacLeod, J. (1993) *Community Organising: A Practical and Theological Appraisal* (London: Christian Action)

Martin, S. (1990) *Community Work, Community Organising and the Challenge for the Church*, paper written for Merseyside Sponsoring Group's Working Party (Merseyside Churches' Urban Institute)

Meekosha, H. (1993) 'The Bodies Politic – Equality, Difference and Community Practice' in ed. H. Butcher, A. Glen, P. Henderson, and J. Smith, *Community and Public Policy* (London: Pluto Press CDF/BICC), pp. 171–193

Merseyside Churches' Urban Institute (1991) *Broad Based Organising on Merseyside*, Working Party Report (Liverpool: MCUI)

Pitt, J. and Keane, M. (1984) *Community Organising? You've Never Really Tried It!* (Birmingham: J & P Consultancy)

Radford, J. (1978) 'Don't Agonise – Organise' in ed. P. Curno, *Political Issues and Community Work* (London: Routledge & Kegan Paul), pp. 106–119

Twelvetrees, A. (1986) 'Lessons from America – Alinsky's Legacy' in *Community Care*, 22 May 1986

Twelvetrees, A. (1988) 'Community Work, Community Organising and the Role of the Worker' in *Christian Action Journal* (London: Christian Action), pp. 6–7